The First Course

Rick Stromoski

**Andrews McMeel
Publishing**

Kansas City

ISBN: 0-7407-3946-8

Library of Congress Control Number: 2003100766

03 04 05 06 07 BBG 10 9 8 7 6 5 4 3 2 1

──────── **ATTENTION: SCHOOLS AND BUSINESSES** ────────

Andrews McMeel books are available at quantity discounts with bulk purchase for educational, business, or sales promotional use. For information, please write to: Special Sales Department, Andrews McMeel Publishing, 4520 Main Street, Kansas City, Missouri 64111.

For Chucky, Bobby, Debbie, Becky, Tommy, Judy, Barbara, Raymond, Joseph, Stephen, and David.

And Mom and Dad.

Foreword

Each spring, America's top cartoonists gather for the National Cartoonists Society Awards Weekend and honor the nation's outstanding artists of the year.

His peers already know how inventive and innovative Rick Stromoski is (because we have heard his inspired excuses for not buying a round of drinks at the bar).

We already find him screamingly funny (for we have seen him squeezed into his tiny bathing suit, wallowing in many a hotel pool).

And we cartoonists already know just how brilliantly Rick Stromoski cartoons . . . that's why the members of the NCS have nominated him as Outstanding Artist of the Year on eleven occasions, in five separate divisions from Book Illustration to Greeting Cards. (He has won three times—twice for greeting cards and once for his gag cartoon work.)

His daily comic strip *Soup to Nutz* is wonderfully observed, beautifully drawn, and invariably laugh-out-loud funny. Each morning, it gives the readers of our nation's newspapers the chance to learn what the world's top cartoonists already know . . . that Rick Stromoski is tightfisted and looks ridiculous in a Speedo.

Steve McGarry,
President,
National Cartoonists Society

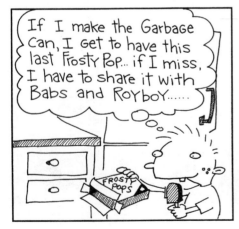

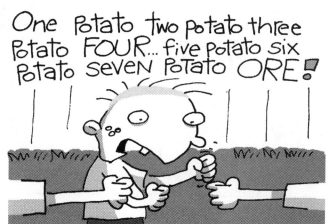

19

27

47

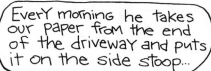

50

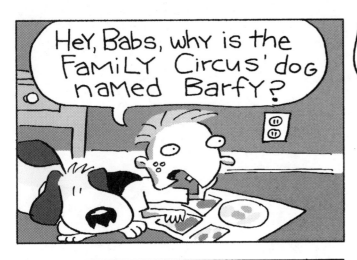

60

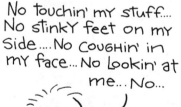

Hi, Mom....

Perfectly Good Apeman mask.... THROWN into the GARBAGE!!!

—STroMoski—

Gross... Is that the old, left-over, stale peanut brittle from the back of the pantry?

Yup.

Crunch! Crunch! Crunch!

Can I have some?

Nope.

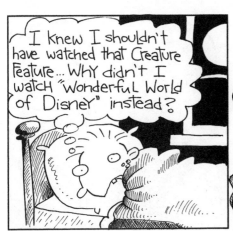

I knew I shouldn't have watched that Creature Feature... Why didn't I watch "Wonderful World of Disney" instead?

They're not really there.... They're not really there.....

—STroMoski—

75

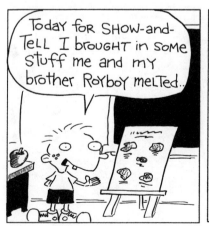

96

105